Table of Content

MW00522655

Read the passage. Then answer questions 1–10.

Publishing Night

1   Emma's class had been preparing for Publishing Night for weeks. The fourth grade class had worked on revision after revision of poems. Now they had clean, polished copies of their final drafts. These final copies were free of the scrawled notations of their peers and Mr. Thomas's words of advice and encouragement.

2   A professional bookbinder helped the students bind their poems into hardcover books. Emma gazed at her name printed neatly on the cover. She had a feeling this was one assignment she would keep forever.

3   Emma knew that she had a knack for writing even before the start of this classroom project. She and her father wrote poems together for birthdays, holidays, and other special occasions. Their creations were always a hit with friends and family.

4   Emma asked her father if he'd like to read her poems. "I think I'll wait to hear them when you read aloud at Publishing Night," he answered. Emma could not wait to share her new work with others.

5   On Publishing Night, Emma put on her new blue jumper and set off for school with her parents. It felt so strange to pull into the school driveway at night. Emma could recall only one other special evening at school. She had played one of the lead roles in her class play. Emma smiled as she remembered the roar of the applause.

continued →

6   That smile quickly faded and Emma paled. Tonight she would not be playing a part and reading lines someone else had written. She glanced down at her own name on the book she held. She would be alone up there on stage reading her own words for all to hear.

7   Emma's stomach churned as teachers, parents, and students took their seats in the auditorium. Before long, it was her turn to take the stage. She opened the book with trembling fingers. Her tongue felt dry and swollen in her mouth. Emma held her book in front of her face, hoping to block the mass of strangers from view. Her cheeks grew red. As she opened her mouth to read, her throat constricted. Emma could not utter a sound! After a few excruciating minutes on the stage, Mr. Thomas gave her a comforting pat on the back and guided Emma back to her parents.

5

8   On the way home, Emma sat alone in the back seat. Finally she could no longer bear the silence. "Why couldn't I read my poems like all the other kids?" she wailed. "They're going to make fun of me now!"

9   Later, Emma's dad asked her to read the poems to him. At first, Emma said, "No way. I never want to see those poems again!" After a soothing cup of hot milk, Emma calmed down. She agreed to read aloud. After hearing the poems, her parents eventually persuaded her to try reading aloud to her class, a much smaller group than the Publishing Night audience.

10   The next day, Emma presented her idea to Mr. Thomas. When the time came for her to read, her classmates recalled Emma's stage fright the night before. They wondered what would happen this time. When Emma began, her confidence amazed her classmates. Emma beamed as she heard their heartfelt applause. It seemed even more enthusiastic than any cheer she had heard in the auditorium the night before.

continued

1. This question has two parts. Answer Part A first. Then answer Part B.

Part A How does Emma feel near the beginning of the passage?

    A embarrassed about her poems

    B happy to be done with her book at last

    C proud of her poetry

    D bored from revising her poems so many times

Part B Which detail from the passage supports the answer to Part A?

    A The class had been working for weeks.

    B The students revised their work many times.

    C The final copies had no notes or scribbles.

    D Emma thought she would always keep the book of poems.

2. This question has two parts. Answer Part A first. Then answer Part B.

Part A What is the meaning of the word <u>constricted</u> in paragraph 7?

    A became quiet

    B blushed

    C shrank; closed up

    D made a humming noise

Part B Which sentence from paragraph 7 helps you understand the meaning of <u>constricted</u>?

    A Before long, it was her turn to take the stage.

    B She opened the book with trembling fingers.

    C Emma held her book in front of her face, hoping to block the mass of strangers from view.

    D Emma could not utter a sound!

continued

3. In the illustration that goes with the passage, who is the man on the stage behind Emma?

    A   Emma's father

    B   Mr. Thomas

    C   the school principal

    D   the bookbinder

4. Which sentence **best** describes how Emma probably feels at the end of the passage?

    A   She feels upset because Mr. Thomas would not give her a second chance to read her poems.

    B   She feels proud to make a comeback after a difficult experience.

    C   She is glad she will never have to read in public again.

    D   She is pleased to show her classmates that her work is better than theirs.

5. Choose three details from the passage that the author uses to show how Emma feels as she tries to read at Publishing Night. Check the box next to each detail you choose.

❑   Her stomach churns unpleasantly when she sees the audience.

❑   She has trouble remembering other special occasions at school.

❑   Her fingers tremble.

❑   She wants to keep her book as a treasure rather than read her poems aloud.

❑   She cries and refuses to read the poems.

❑   Her tongue feels dry and swollen in her mouth.

❑   The roar of the applause startles her.

6. Choose two inferences you can make from the passage about Emma's relationship with her parents. Check the box next to each inference you choose.

❑   Emma enjoys working on poems with her father.

❑   Emma's parents wish she would work harder on her school projects.

❑   Emma does not like sharing her work with her parents.

❑   Emma's parents are embarrassed when she can't read her poems.

❑   Emma refuses to listen to her parents' advice.

❑   Emma's parents want her to experience success with her poems.

continued

7. Choose four sentences that should be included in a summary of the passage and number them in the correct order.

—— Students in Emma's class revise their stories and poems many times.

—— Emma reads her poems in class the next day.

—— Emma's cheeks grow pale.

—— Emma suffers stage fright and cannot read her poems aloud at Publishing Night.

—— The audience looks frightening to Emma.

—— One time, Emma acted in her school play.

—— Emma looks forward to reading her poems at Publishing Night.

—— Emma's classmates cheer for her after she reads her poems.

8. Why does Emma become anxious as she approaches the auditorium on Publishing Night? Use details from the passage to support your response.

_____

_____

_____

_____

_____

9. Why does Emma at first refuse to read her poems after she returns home from Publishing Night? Use details from the passage to support your answer.

_____

_____

_____

_____

_____

continued ➡

12

10. What important lessons does Emma probably learn from her experience? Use at least three details from the passage to support your response.

_____

_____

_____

_____

_____

_____

_____

_____

_____

_____

Read the passage. Then answer questions 1–10.

Out There

1   Ammy didn't sleep a wink the night before leaving. How could she? She and her friend Calix were about to embark on a journey to save the entire colony of Sub Terran. Who *could* sleep at a time like this? She wondered if Calix suffered from insomnia that night too. He was such a worrier! Ammy could just imagine him tossing and turning all night. She wondered why the Elders even chose Calix, but then decided it didn't matter as long as the mission succeeded.

2   Ammy remembered the night she and Calix had been summoned to the Elder Cave. It was a round, enormous room with walls of smooth blue limestone. Towers of pale yellow stone lined the entrance. Hundreds of pure white stalactites hung from the ceiling and glistened in the damp air. They reminded Ammy of so many giant bat teeth. The cave was intimidating, to say the least.

3   One of the Elders had explained, "As you both know, our colony has outgrown the tunnels and caves of Sub Terran. Our history tells us of a place of great space, clean air, warm light, and something called *sky.* You, Amethyst Stone and Calix Spar, have been chosen to find this place known as *Out There* and determine if our people can live there safely."

continued ➤

4   Calix began to fret immediately. "But why us?" he whined. "Why not choose someone older and stronger to make such a perilous journey? Surely the risks are too great for two twelve-year-old children!"

5   "Your young bodies have not permanently adapted to life underground and can handle the elements you are likely to face. We need you to find something to bring back to prove that Out There exists and can house our people."

6   "How will we know what to select?" Ammy asked.

7   "Find something that holds the promise of life."

8   Now that it was time to leave for Out There, even Ammy felt nervous. "Nothing to do but go," she muttered. She adjusted her headlamp, tied a rope around her backpack just in case, and set off to meet Calix.

9   Calix looked anxious. "Come on, Calix," Ammy reassured him. "It'll be fun! Just think—we leave as children, but we'll come back as heroes!" She offered a bright, confident smile. Calix couldn't help but smile back.

10   They traveled for three days. The sights were amazing. Glistening crystals studded smooth pink walls. Cave spiders' pale bodies blended neatly with rippled yellow flow stone. When the children came to an underground lake, Ammy couldn't resist—she just had to get her feet wet.

11   "I don't think that's a good idea," warned Calix. "We should keep moving. Plus, you don't know how deep that water is, and I'm *not* coming in to save you!"

12   "Relax," Ammy said as she stepped farther in. "I can see the bottom. There will be no swimming for you today, I promise!"

13 Ammy cried out as she slipped suddenly beneath the water. In an instant, Calix understood: *Ammy slipped on the smooth bottom into deeper water, and she doesn't know how to swim.* But instead of panicking, Calix seized Ammy's rope and tied one end to a stalagmite and the other around his waist. He waded carefully into the water to where his friend flailed in the water. Calix held her with one arm and pulled them both along the rope toward safety.

14 "Calix!" gasped Ammy. "You saved me! Thank you!"

15 "I did save you, didn't I?" replied Calix. Even *he* couldn't believe it. He stood a little taller, cleared his throat, and said, "Ammy, dry off and let's find Out There."

16 It wasn't long before the air felt cooler and smelled sweeter. "Look!" shouted Ammy. She pointed to a light at the end of the tunnel. They rushed forward and then froze; they were standing in the very mouth of the cave. Behind them was the darkness of Sub Terran. Before them was the dazzling world of Out There.

17 Calix took Ammy by the hand. They stepped into the sunlight and stood in awe. Such colors and sounds! A million emerald leaves whispered overhead, blossoms of white, violet, and indigo buzzed with fuzzy yellow insects.

18 "What *is* that?" Ammy asked, pointing to the brilliant blue ceiling. It was so high, with no end in sight.

19 "The sky!" Calix exclaimed. "Ammy, we did it! We have found Out There!"

20 "We still need to choose something to bring back," Ammy whispered, "something to prove this world is safe and real and alive." She looked all around. How could she know what to choose? The Elder's words echoed in her mind. *Find something that holds the promise of life.* Ammy walked over to a cluster of ferns and picked a fiddlehead. She could tell that it was the bud of a young fern that had not yet opened. "Here," she said. "This will do. What could hold more promise than this?"

continued ➞

1. This question has two parts. Answer Part A first. Then answer Part B.

Part A What is the meaning of the word <u>perilous</u> in paragraph 4?

    A worrisome

    B weak

    C lengthy

    D dangerous

Part B Which sentence from the passage helps you understand the meaning of <u>perilous</u>?

    A "Our history tells us of a place of great space, clean air, warm light, and something called *sky*."

    B Calix began to fret immediately.

    C "But why us?" he whined.

    D "Surely the risks are too great for two twelve-year-old children!"

2. Based on the way she acts around Calix, what can you infer about Ammy?

    A Ammy likes Calix and wants to impress him.

    B Ammy is competitive and hopes to show Calix up.

    C Ammy acts positive, even though she feels nervous.

    D Ammy is unaware of any danger, so she acts foolishly.

3. How would this story be different if it were told in the first person from Calix's point of view?

    A The reader would learn more of Calix's inner thoughts and feelings.

    B The reader would learn Ammy's true feelings about Calix.

    C The reader would learn more details about the people of Sub Terran.

    D The reader would have a better understanding of the problems in Sub Terran.

continued ➤

4. This question has two parts. Answer Part A first. Then answer Part B.

Part A Which sentence expresses a theme of this passage?

A   Life in a sunless world is difficult and dangerous.

B   There is great promise and strength in even the smallest things.

C   Always pack a rope when going on an adventure.

D   If you want to succeed at something, ask a friend to help.

Part B Which detail from the passage supports the answer to Part A?

A   Although Ammy begins the adventure bravely, her friend is actually the hero.

B   The children plan ahead so they don't have problems on their adventure.

C   The children bring a small plant back to Sub Terran to show the promise of Out There.

D   The children willingly accept the challenge in order to help their colony.

5. Choose two inferences you can make about Calix, based on the passage. Check the box next to each inference you choose.

   ❑   He and Ammy have been enemies since childhood.

   ❑   He finds it easy to put worries out of his mind.

   ❑   He feels the Elders were right in choosing him and Ammy to find Out There.

   ❑   He prefers to take the safe route whenever possible.

   ❑   He is always craving the next adventure.

   ❑   He would risk his own life to save Ammy.

6. Choose three sentences from the passage that suggest the setting of the story is very different from our world. Check the box next to each sentence you choose.

   ❑   Ammy could just imagine him tossing and turning all night.

   ❑   It was a round, enormous room with walls of smooth blue limestone.

   ❑   "Our history tells us of a place of great space, clean air, warm light, and something called *sky*."

   ❑   "Find something that holds the promise of life."

   ❑   When the children came to an underground lake, Ammy couldn't resist—she just had to get her feet wet.

   ❑   She adjusted her headlamp, tied a rope around her backpack just in case, and set off to meet Calix.

   ❑   It wasn't long before the air felt cooler and smelled sweeter.

   ❑   "What *is* that?" Ammy asked, pointing to the brilliant blue ceiling.

continued ➤

7. Choose four sentences that should be included in a summary of this passage and number them in the correct order.

— Two twelve-year-old children, Ammy and Calix, are chosen to find Out There.

— Life underground is dark, and many strange creatures live there.

— The colony of Sub Terran is too large and needs to find a new place to live.

— Ammy stops at an underground lake to get her feet wet.

— Calix does not sleep well the night before setting off on the adventure.

— The children find Out There and discover it holds promise as a new home for the colony.

— Ammy and Calix travel for three days together.

— Calix worries about many things.

8. What character traits make Ammy a good choice for the mission to find Out There? Use details from the passage to explain.

_____

_____

_____

_____

_____

9. Why does Ammy pick a fiddlehead from a fern to take back to the Elders? Use details from the passage to support your answer.

_____

_____

_____

_____

_____

continued

10. Explain why the scene in which Calix saves Ammy from the lake is a turning point for both characters. Include at least three details from the passage to support your response.

_____

_____

_____

_____

_____

_____

_____

_____

_____

_____

Short Read 3 • Folktale

Read the passage. Then answer questions 1–10.

How the Bluebird Got Its Color

Told by the Pima Indians (Arizona)
(Source: The Project Gutenberg E-Book *Myths and Legends of California and the Old Southwest*, edited by Katharine Berry Judson)

1   A long time ago, the bluebird was a very ugly color. But Bluebird knew of a lake where no river flowed in or out, and he bathed in this four times every morning for four days. Each time, he sang a secret song:

2   *Here is a lake with water so blue,*

3   *In four days' time, my feathers will be new.*

4   On the fourth morning, Bluebird shed all his feathers and came out of the lake in just his skin. Then the next morning, when he came out of the lake, he was covered with blue feathers!

continued ➤

5   Now all this while, Coyote had been watching Bluebird. Coyote wanted to jump in and get Bluebird to eat, but Coyote was afraid of the water. Still, on that last morning Coyote said, "How is it you have lost all your dull color, and now you are a vivid, beautiful blue? You are more beautiful than anything that flies in the air. I want to be blue, too." Now at that time, Coyote was a bright green.

6   "I only went in four times on four mornings," said Bluebird. He taught Coyote the secret song; Coyote went in four times, and the last time he came out as blue as the little bird.

7   Then Coyote was very, very proud of his new blue fur. He was so proud that as he walked along, he glanced around on every side to see if anybody was looking at him to admire how beautiful he was. He looked to see if his shadow was blue too.

8   Coyote was so busy watching to see if others were noticing him that he did not watch the trail. By and by, he ran so hard into a stump that he fell down in the dirt, and he was covered all over with dust. You may know this is true because even today, coyotes are the color of dirt.

1. Which sentence **best** explains the importance of the story setting?

   A   Bluebird and Coyote sing a secret song by the lake.

   B   Coyote learns to swim in the water of the lake.

   C   Bluebird and Coyote change color in the lake.

   D   Coyote is afraid to go into the water.

2. What is Coyote's interest in Bluebird at the beginning of the story?

   A   Coyote hopes that Bluebird will teach him to swim.

   B   Coyote wants to use Bluebird's feathers for a new coat.

   C   Coyote wants to learn Bluebird's beauty secret.

   D   Coyote hopes to eat Bluebird.

continued

3. This question has two parts. Answer Part A first. Then answer Part B.

Part A What is the meaning of the word <u>vivid</u> in paragraph 5?

    A glad

    B bright

    C delicious

    D interesting

Part B Which phrase from paragraph 5 helps you understand the meaning of <u>vivid</u>?

    A afraid of the water

    B that last morning

    C lost all your dull color

    D anything that flies in the air

4. What is the main theme of this passage?

    A Too much pride may bring you trouble.

    B The ability to laugh at yourself is a great gift.

    C Appearances are not important, after all.

    D He who laughs last, laughs best.

5. Choose four sentences that belong in a summary of this passage and number them in the correct order.

— Coyote was afraid of water.

— Bluebird's feathers turned blue.

— Bluebird bathed in a lake and sang a secret song four times.

— Bluebird wanted to change his color.

— Bluebird was nothing but skin.

— Coyote was once bright green.

— Coyote turned his fur blue but then lost his new color.

6. Choose two inferences you can make from the illustration in the passage. Check the box next to each inference you choose.

❑ Bluebird is excited about his new color.

❑ Bluebird and Coyote have been friends for a long time.

❑ Coyote is afraid of the water.

❑ Coyote looks at Bluebird as a nice meal, not a friend.

❑ Coyote does not know how to swim.

❑ Coyote thinks of himself as very handsome.

continued ➡

7. If this story were turned into a play, which new elements would be added? Choose three elements that would be added and check the box next to each element.

❑ character development

❑ a setting

❑ a cast of characters

❑ dialogue

❑ stage directions

❑ stanzas

❑ acts or scenes

8. Does Coyote get what he deserves? Use details from the passage to support your answer.

_____

_____

_____

_____

_____

_____

9. This story is a Native American pourquoi tale that explains how certain things in nature came to be. What two things in nature does this story explain?

_____

_____

_____

_____

_____

_____

continued →

10. What makes Bluebird decide to teach Coyote his secret song, and what happens as a result? Use at least three details from the passage in your answer.

_____

_____

_____

_____

_____

_____

_____

_____

_____

_____

_____

Short Read 4 • Drama

Read the passage. Then answer questions 1–10.

Heidi

Adapted from the novel by Johanna Spyri

Cast of Characters:

HEIDI, a girl from the mountains of Switzerland

CLARA, a twelve-year-old girl living in Frankfurt, Germany

GRANDMAMA, Clara's grandmother

PETER, Heidi's best friend at home in the mountains

1   *Setting:* HEIDI *is living for a short time with her friend,* CLARA, *in Frankfurt. In this scene,* HEIDI *is sitting with* GRANDMAMA *in the living room of* CLARA'S *home. The two are looking at a book.* HEIDI *is bent over the book, eagerly looking at the illustrations. Suddenly, her eyes open wide with wonder and surprise, and she lets out a joyful scream.* HEIDI *places her hand upon an illustration showing a peaceful flock of sheep grazing in a beautiful green pasture, a kind-looking shepherd leaning on his crook beneath a tree.* HEIDI'S *eyes fill with tears, and her screams of delight suddenly turn to sobs of sorrow.*

2   **GRANDMAMA:** *(soothingly and lovingly)* Come, child, you must not cry. Did this remind you of something? Now stop, and I'll tell you the story tonight. There are lovely stories in this book that people can read and tell. Dry your tears now, darling. I must ask you something. Stand up now and look at me! Now we are merry again!

3   HEIDI *continues to cry for some time.* GRANDMAMA *waits patiently, places an arm around* HEIDI'S *shoulders, and gives her time to stop crying.* HEIDI *slowly begins to calm down.*

4   **GRANDMAMA:** *(kindly)* Now it's all over. Now we'll be merry again.

5   HEIDI *finally stops crying and turns her tear-streaked face up toward* GRANDMAMA.

continued

6 **GRANDMAMA:** Tell me now how your lessons are going. What have you learnt, child?

7 **HEIDI:** *(quietly, as if ashamed)* Nothing, but I knew that I never could learn it.

8 **GRANDMAMA:** What is it that you can't learn?

9 **HEIDI:** *(quietly)* I can't learn to read; it is too hard.

10 **GRANDMAMA:** *(looking surprised)* What next? Who gave you this information?

11 **HEIDI:** Peter told me, and he tried over and over again, but he could not do it, for it is too hard.

12 GRANDMAMA *sighs. Her eyes and voice soften and she gently turns* HEIDI'S *face to hers so she can look* HEIDI *right in the eyes.*

13 **GRANDMAMA:** Well, what kind of boy is he? Heidi, you must not believe what Peter tells you, but try for yourself. I am sure you had your thoughts elsewhere when Mr. Candidate showed you the letters.

14 **HEIDI:** *(sounding defeated as if she is resigned to her fate)* It's no use.

15 HEIDI'S *eyes fill with tears again and her chin starts to quiver.* GRANDMAMA *hugs* HEIDI *tighter and continues patiently.*

16 **GRANDMAMA:** I am going to tell you something, Heidi. You have not learnt to read because you have believed what Peter said. You shall believe me now, and I prophesy that you will learn it in a very short time, as a great many other children do that are like you and not like Peter.

17 HEIDI *listens attentively and begins to sit taller in*
    GRANDMAMA'S *arms. A small smile begins to form on her face*
    and a glimmer of hope begins to flicker in her eyes.

18 **GRANDMAMA:** When you can read, I am going to give you
    this book. You have seen the shepherd in the green pasture,
    and then you'll be able to find out all the strange things that
    happen to him. Yes, you can hear the whole story, and what
    he does with his sheep and his goats. You would like to know,
    wouldn't you, Heidi?

19 HEIDI'S *eyes sparkle as she listens to* GRANDMAMA, *and her*
    smile brightens her face like the sun. She places her arms
    around GRANDMAMA'S *neck.*

20 **HEIDI:** *(bubbling with excitement)* If only I could read already!

21 **GRANDMAMA:** *(laughing and hugging* HEIDI *in return)* It
    won't be long, I can see that. Come now and let us go to Clara.

22 HEIDI *gently closes the book.* GRANDMAMA *slowly rises from*
    her seat, takes HEIDI'S *hand in hers, and they walk out of the*
    room in search of CLARA.

continued

1. Read the sentence from the play.

> You shall believe me now, and I <u>prophesy</u> that you will learn it in a very short time, as a great many other children do that are like you and not like Peter.

What is the meaning of the word <u>prophesy</u>?

    A bet

    B predict

    C hope

    D doubt

2. This question has two parts. Answer Part A first. Then answer Part B.

Part A How successful was Peter in learning to read?

    A He learned to read easily and quickly.

    B He worked hard and now can read.

    C He learned to read some words but does not understand them.

    D He tried for a long time but found reading too difficult.

Part B Which sentence from the play supports the answer in Part A?

    A "Peter told me, and he tried over and over again, but he could not do it, for it is too hard."

    B "Well, what kind of boy is he?"

    C "I am sure you had your thoughts elsewhere when Mr. Candidate showed you the letters."

    D "It won't be long, I can see that."

3. Toward the end of the passage, Heidi's "eyes sparkle as she listens to Grandmama." What does this phrase suggest about Heidi?

    A She cries a lot when Grandmama speaks.

    B She has tears in her eyes.

    C She is excited about learning to read.

    D She feels angry about what Peter told her.

4. This question has two parts. Answer Part A first. Then answer Part B.

Part A What is the theme, or message, in this passage?

    A Older people, like Grandmama, give the best advice.

    B Books with pictures are the best kind for children to read.

    C Children should not cry just because something is difficult.

    D Don't let other people's failures keep you from succeeding.

Part B Which sentence from the passage supports the answer in Part A?

    A "Come, child, you must not cry."

    B "Heidi, you must not believe what Peter tells you, but try for yourself."

    C "I am going to tell you something, Heidi."

    D "When you can read, I am going to give you this book."

continued ➤

5. Which four sentences belong in a summary of this passage from Heidi? Choose the four sentences and number them in the correct order.

—— Heidi and Peter are childhood friends.

—— Heidi trusts Grandmama and believes her encouraging words.

—— Grandmama doesn't like to see children cry.

—— Heidi decides to not let Peter's difficult experience learning to read stop her from trying.

—— Heidi thinks that because Peter could not learn how to read, she won't be able to either.

—— Heidi loves books about sheep and green pastures.

—— Grandmama knows that once Heidi believes she can learn how to read, she will.

—— Grandmama gives crying children plenty of time to calm down.

6. How does Heidi's attitude about reading change from the beginning of the passage to the end? Choose two lines from the play that show how she felt about reading at the beginning and two lines that show how she felt at the end. Write a 1 next to the lines from the beginning and write a 2 next to the lines from the end.

—   "There are lovely stories in this book that people can read and tell."

—   "Nothing, but I knew that I never could learn it."

—   "I can't learn to read; it is too hard."

—   "I am sure you had your thoughts elsewhere when Mr. Candidate showed you the letters."

—   GRANDMAMA *hugs* HEIDI *tighter and continues patiently.*

—   "You have not learnt to read because you have believed what Peter said."

—   HEIDI *listens attentively and begins to sit taller in* GRANDMAMA'S *arms.*

—   "When you can read, I am going to give you this book."

—   "Yes, you can hear the whole story, and what he does with his sheep and his goats."

—   HEIDI'S *eyes sparkle as she listens to* GRANDMAMA, *and her smile brightens her face like the sun.*

—   "If only I could read already!"

continued

7. How is this play different from a story or poem on the same subject? Check the box beside each sentence that describes a feature of the play that would not be found in a story or poem.

☐   It takes place in a certain setting.

☐   It uses words that rhyme.

☐   It includes stage directions.

☐   It is organized in acts and scenes.

☐   It has a certain rhythm and meter.

☐   It includes dialogue.

☐   It has events in a plot.

☐   It lists a cast of characters.

8. How does Grandmama help change Heidi's mind about learning to read? Use details from the play to support your answer.

_____

_____

_____

_____

_____

9. How does the illustration of Grandmama and Heidi add to the reader's enjoyment and understanding of this passage? Give at least two examples in your answer.

_____

_____

_____

_____

continued

40

10. Imagine that this scene from the play was told in the first person from Heidi's or Grandmama's point of view. Describe how this scene would be different if it were narrated in the first person by Heidi or Grandmama. Use at least three details from the passage to support your answer.

_____

_____

_____

_____

_____

_____

_____

_____

_____

_____

Read the passage. Then answer questions 1–10.

The Monarch Butterfly: Nature's Timekeeper

1   Our natural world has certain rhythms. Night turns into day. Ocean tides rise and fall. Seasons change as Earth spins on its axis. There are also rhythms in every culture, even in our daily lives. We get up for school or work each day. We eat our meals in a certain order. We celebrate holidays at the same time each year.

2   Nature may not need help keeping its rhythms, but we humans do. For this reason, we invented things such as clocks and calendars to help guide us. But inventions such as these have not always been around, so how did ancient people keep track of time and natural cycles? One surprising answer to this question is butterflies—the monarch butterfly, to be exact.

continued

3   As its name suggests, the monarch is the "king" or "queen" of all butterflies. Every year, the monarchs living in eastern Canada and the eastern United States face a life-or-death situation. These butterflies cannot survive cold temperatures. They must find a warm, safe place to live for the winter. In late September or October every year, millions of monarch butterflies leave their eastern homes and fly south to the *oyamel* forests in central Mexico. These forests of balsam fir trees make the ideal sanctuary for millions of monarchs that migrate there year after year.

4   The butterflies' trip to Mexico is 2,000 to 3,000 miles long. How do these fragile creatures fly so far? Don't let the monarch's delicate appearance fool you. This butterfly is one tough insect. It can fly up to 12 miles per hour, travel up to 30 miles in one day, and fly at heights of up to 2 miles. This amazing insect can even fly across the Atlantic Ocean. That is one strong butterfly!

5   Hundreds of years ago, the people in this part of Mexico, called Michoacán (mee-choh-ah-KAHN), saw the monarchs arrive. They admired these stunning creatures and looked forward to their arrival each year. But how did the monarch butterfly help people keep track of time? The people noticed a pattern in the rhythm of the monarchs' arrival and departure. When the butterflies arrived in early November, it was time to harvest the corn and other crops. When the butterflies left in early March, it was time to plant.

6   Year after year, the people watched and waited. They harvested and planted according to the monarch's migration pattern, and the system worked well. The monarch became an important and beloved creature to the people of Michoacán, and the people honored the monarch for helping them grow enough food. In fact, the people still hold local festivals each year that pay tribute to the monarch. They play music and dance to celebrate the butterflies and the harvest.

7   The return of the monarchs is also important to Mexican culture. The Mexican holiday *Día de los Muertos* (or "Day of the Dead") takes place on November 2, as the monarchs arrive. On this day, people pay respect to loved ones who have died. According to Mexican folklore, the butterflies carry ancestors' spirits back to their homeland in Michoacán. Images of the monarch can be seen in paintings, decorations, and homes. Several other festivals honor the monarchs as they begin to leave Mexico and return to the North.

8   Today the monarch butterfly is still a treasured and respected creature in Michoacán. But modern life threatens the butterfly's survival. Its habitat has been threatened because people have cut down the trees for lumber and other uses. Without the *oyamel* forests, the monarchs would have no winter home, so the Mexican government passed a law. Since 1986, it has been illegal to cut down or harm these forests in any way. This law has helped the monarchs survive and follow their natural cycles. And the monarchs have long helped the people of Michoacán.

continued ➡

44

1. This question has two parts. Answer Part A first. Then answer Part B.

Part A What is the meaning of the word <u>sanctuary</u> in paragraph 3?

    A goal or destination

    B threatened habitat

    C safe place to stay

    D secret life

Part B Which sentence from the passage helps you understand the meaning of <u>sanctuary</u>?

    A As its name suggests, the monarch is the "king" or "queen" of all butterflies.

    B Every year, the monarchs living in eastern Canada and the eastern United States face a life-or-death situation.

    C These butterflies cannot survive cold temperatures.

    D They must find a warm, safe place to live for the winter.

2. Why were monarch butterflies so important to the ancient people of Michoacán?

   A The butterflies spread joy to everyone with their beauty and grace.

   B The butterflies helped the people know when to plant and harvest crops.

   C The butterflies helped the people understand their ancestors.

   D The butterflies ate insects that damaged important crops.

3. Why does the author of this passage call the monarch butterfly "nature's timekeeper"?

   A Ancient people knew that the life of the monarch lasted twelve months.

   B The patterns on the monarchs' wings looked like calendars or clocks.

   C People believed that the monarchs brought messages from their ancestors.

   D People used the monarchs' migration cycle as a guide for planting and harvesting crops.

continued

4. This question has two parts. Answer Part A first. Then answer Part B.

Part A Which sentence **best** states the main idea of the passage?

   A   The monarch butterfly is an incredible insect that helped guide the people of Michoacán in their farming.

   B   Without clocks or calendars, people all around the world would not be able to survive.

   C   Monarch butterflies fly thousands of miles every year to survive the winter months.

   D   The *oyamel* forests in Mexico are so important to the monarch that they are protected by law.

Part B Which sentence supports the answer to Part A?

   A   Hundreds of years ago, the people in this part of Mexico, called Michoacán (mee-choh-ah-KAHN), saw the monarchs arrive.

   B   They admired these stunning creatures and looked forward to their arrival each year.

   C   They harvested and planted according to the monarch's migration pattern, and the system worked well.

   D   In fact, the people still hold local festivals each year that pay tribute to the monarch.

5. Choose three inferences you can make about the monarch butterfly based on the passage. Check the box next to each inference you choose.

❏ The monarch has great strength and endurance for its size.

❏ The monarch is becoming less important to the people of Mexico each year.

❏ The holiday called *Día de Los Muertos* began as a way to honor the monarchs.

❏ The monarch's survival matters greatly to the people of Michoacán.

❏ Monarch butterflies have no places to live in the United States.

❏ The monarch is an important part of Michoacán history and culture.

❏ The state of Michoacán would not survive without the monarch.

6. Choose three sentences the author uses to show the importance of the monarch butterfly to the people of Michoacán. Check the box next to each sentence you choose.

❏ Several other festivals honor the monarchs as they begin to leave Mexico and return to the North.

❏ They harvested and planted according to the monarch's migration pattern, and the system worked well.

❏ This amazing insect can even fly across the Atlantic Ocean.

❏ One surprising answer to this question is butterflies—the monarch butterfly, to be exact.

❏ These forests of balsam fir trees make the ideal sanctuary for millions of monarchs that migrate there year after year.

❏ Without the *oyamel* forests, the monarchs would have no winter home, so the Mexican government passed a law.

continued ➤

7. The chart below lists four causes. Choose the effect that fits each cause. Write the letter in the Effects column next to each cause.

Causes	Effects
Humans needed help keeping track of natural cycles.	
The monarchs could not survive cold temperatures.	
The people of Michoacán saw the monarchs arrive in the fall.	
In early November, the people of Michoacán honored the monarchs.	

A The monarchs flew south to Mexico each year.

B The monarch is the "king" or "queen" of all butterflies.

C People invented clocks and calendars.

D Images of the monarch appeared in paintings, decorations, and homes.

E Monarch butterflies traveled up to thirty miles per day.

F The people harvested their corn and other crops.

G People began cutting down trees in the *oyamel* forests.

8. What evidence does the author give to support the idea that the people of Michoacán still honor the monarch butterfly? Give at least two details from the text to support your answer.

_____

_____

_____

_____

_____

9. How do the photographs help readers better understand the information presented in the passage? Give two examples.

_____

_____

_____

_____

_____

continued ➤

10. How do the monarchs and the people of Michoacán depend on and help each other? Use at least four details from the passage to support your answer.

_____

_____

_____

_____

_____

_____

_____

_____

_____

_____

Read the passage. Then answer questions 1–10.

George Gershwin: The Music of America

1   *Jacob Gershowitz* may not be a household name, but he is one of the most famous American composers of all time. He was better known as George Gershwin. George was born in Brooklyn, New York, in 1898, the second of four children. Both of his parents had emigrated from Russia.

2   Music played an important role in the Gershwin household. George's parents bought a piano for his brother, Ira, when he was a boy. However, it was George who was drawn to the instrument at an early age. Gershwin quickly learned to play the piano very well. At the age of fifteen, he left school and got a job playing music in New York City.

continued

3   Gershwin worked as a "song plugger" in Tin Pan Alley. That was the center of the music industry in New York City. It was probably named for the tinny sound of cheap pianos. Song pluggers spent their workday playing popular songs on piano in music shops. Their music encouraged customers to buy sheet music from the store. This job improved Gershwin's skills as a musician. It also helped him learn the popular music of the era.

4   It was not long before Gershwin began writing his own music. He published his first song when he was only seventeen years old. His first big hit came in 1919 with the song "Swanee." The catchy song sold around two million records and one million copies of sheet music.

5   In the 1920s, Gershwin began experimenting with different kinds of music. He wrote two of his most famous compositions in this period. In 1924 he completed *Rhapsody in Blue,* a composition for solo piano and jazz band. Then he traveled to France to study music with European composers. When he returned, he wrote *An American in Paris*.

6   Over the years, George's brother Ira became his main lyricist, often writing the words to George's tunes. The Gershwin brothers collaborated on many musical comedies. In 1935 the brothers wrote the American folk opera *Porgy and Bess.* At first, this musical was a box office failure, in part because it featured a cast of black performers. That was a controversial decision at the time. But eventually, *Porgy and Bess* became the Gershwins' most highly respected work.

7   After his disappointment with *Porgy and Bess,* George moved to Hollywood. There, he switched gears and started writing music for movies.

8   Gershwin never forgot his roots as a New York City "song plugger" or his love of classical music. Throughout his career, he included popular and traditional folk music in his compositions. Gershwin combined the musical style of African American music with both popular and operatic techniques in *Porgy and Bess*. He blended classical music and jazz in *An American in Paris* and *Rhapsody in Blue*. This secured Gershwin's reputation as one of the greatest composers of the twentieth century.

9   Gershwin's brilliant career was cut short in 1937 when he started to suffer from terrible headaches. Doctors soon discovered that he had a brain tumor. Gershwin continued to work until he collapsed while writing a Hollywood score. He died at the age of thirty-eight.

10   Gershwin once said, "True music must reflect the thought and aspirations of the people and time. My people are Americans. My time is today." Gershwin has been remembered as a musician who captured the true spirit of American culture in the early twentieth century.

continued ➤

1. This question has two parts. Answer Part A first. Then answer Part B.

Part A What is the meaning of the word <u>collaborated</u> in paragraph 6?

    A rediscovered

    B announced loudly

    C worked together

    D advised

Part B Which phrase from paragraph 6 helps you understand the meaning of <u>collaborated</u>?

    A main lyricist

    B writing the words to George's tunes

    C on many musical comedies

    D most highly respected work

2. This question has two parts. Answer Part A first. Then answer Part B.

Part A Which sentence **best** describes Gershwin's musical style?

   A His compositions were strongly influenced by traditional Russian folk music.

   B His music was based mainly on techniques used in opera.

   C His compositions were drawn mainly from popular French songs of the day.

   D His music combined jazz, African American, popular, and classical techniques.

Part B Which paragraph in the passage gives information that supports the answer to Part A?

   A paragraph 2

   B paragraph 3

   C paragraph 4

   D paragraph 8

continued

3. What structure does the author use in this passage to organize and present information?

   A cause and effect

   B chronological order

   C comparison and contrast

   D problem/solution

4. Why was Gershwin disappointed with Porgy and Bess when the show first opened?

   A He did not think it was his best work.

   B He did not work with his brother Ira.

   C He thought it would be better as a movie.

   D It was a box office failure.

5. Choose three events in George Gershwin's life that took place before he had his first big hit, "Swanee." Check the box next to each event you choose.

    ❑   He moved to Hollywood and wrote music for movies.

    ❑   He worked as a "song plugger" in Tin Pan Alley.

    ❑   He suffered from terrible headaches.

    ❑   He quit school.

    ❑   He went to France to study music.

    ❑   He wrote *Rhapsody in Blue*.

    ❑   He published his first song.

6. Choose four sentences that should be included in a summary of this passage and number them in the correct order.

    —   Gershwin's parents came from Russia.

    —   At seventeen years of age, Gershwin published his first song.

    —   Gershwin worked in Hollywood until his death at age thirty-eight.

    —   In the 1920s, Gershwin experimented with different kinds of music and wrote some of his best compositions.

    —   Gershwin was hospitalized with a brain tumor.

    —   George Gershwin quit school at age fifteen and got a job as a "song plugger."

    —   *Porgy and Bess* opened in 1935.

continued ➡

7. Choose two inferences you can make about George Gershwin based on information in the passage. Check the box next to each inference you choose.

   ❑   Gershwin valued the influences of different cultures in his music.

   ❑   Gershwin rebelled against classical European composers.

   ❑   Gershwin was a hardworking composer.

   ❑   Gershwin closely copied the style of his French music teachers.

   ❑   Being a "song plugger" damaged Gershwin's career.

   ❑   Writing music for movies was Gershwin's dream job.

8. According to the author of this passage, was *Porgy and Bess* a success or a failure? Use details from the passage to explain the author's view.

_____

_____

_____

_____

_____

9. How did George's brother Ira help him become successful? Use details from the passage to explain.

_____

_____

_____

_____

_____

continued

10. How did George Gershwin develop his own career through the decisions he made? Use at least three details from the passage to explain how he developed his career.

_____

_____

_____

_____

_____

_____

_____

_____

_____

_____

Read the passage. Then answer questions 1–10.

The First Hot-Air Balloon

1   It's natural to think of manned flight as a modern development, but people first ascended into the sky more than 200 years ago. Human flight began in Paris, France, with a pair of brothers, Joseph and Etienne Montgolfier.

2   One day Joseph discovered something strange. He held the neck of a shirt closed while dangling the garment over a fire, and the shirt billowed upward. He shared the news with his brother. Together, they tried to figure out what had happened. Had the smoke from the fire somehow lifted the shirt?

3   In fact, it was heated air that caused this phenomenon, since hot air rises. As the air heats, it flows upward; as it cools, it flows downward. What the brothers noticed that day would ultimately lead to the first human flight.

continued

4   The Montgolfiers began looking for a way to harness hot air's mysterious power. After much experimentation, they finally created what they called a "balon," a large envelope of cloth and paper. The insides of the balloon were fireproof. When they placed the object over a fire, the balloon rose gracefully—the world's first lighter-than-air craft.

5   On June 5, 1783, the balloon had its first official flight. It reached an altitude of only six feet, but it traveled more than a mile.

6   People were naturally curious about flight. On September 19, 1783, the Montgolfiers set out to prove that living things could fly safely. They did not want to risk a human life, so they "manned" their balloon with animals. The first passengers were a sheep, a rooster, and a duck. The balloon rose over 1,500 feet and traveled for more than two miles. The barnyard passengers were unharmed.

7   The first human passengers flew later that autumn. On November 21, two men, Pilatre de Rozier and the Marquis d'Arlandes, piloted a Montgolfier-built hot-air balloon to more than 2,000 feet. A crowd of 400,000 Parisians watched from the ground below. The flight carried the crew more than five miles in a mere twenty-five minutes. It also carried them into history, along with the Montgolfier brothers.

1. What gave the Montgolfier brothers the idea that led them to construct their first balloon?

   A watching roosters fly

   B noticing a shirt fill up with hot air

   C putting a sheep and a duck in a balloon

   D working with materials such as cloth and paper

2. This question has two parts. Answer Part A first. Then answer Part B.

Part A Which sentence states the main idea of this passage?

   A Many scientific advances depend on the contributions of animals.

   B Human flight began with the work of the Montgolfier brothers.

   C Balloons are capable of incredible feats of aviation.

   D The Montgolfier brothers were superior scientists.

Part B Which sentence from the passage supports the answer to Part A?

   A He shared the news with his brother.

   B Together, they tried to figure out what had happened.

   C Had the smoke from the fire somehow lifted the shirt?

   D When they placed the object over a fire, the balloon rose gracefully—the world's first lighter-than-air craft.

continued →

3. This question has two parts. Answer Part A first. Then answer Part B.

Part A What does the word <u>phenomenon</u> mean in paragraph 3?

    A scientific fact

    B wonderful thing

    C observable event

    D physical impossibility

Part B Which phrase from paragraph 3 helps you understand the meaning of <u>phenomenon</u>?

    A heated air

    B flows downward

    C What the brothers noticed

    D first human flight

4. How does the illustration help you understand the information in the passage?

    A It shows what kind of clothing the men wore in those days.

    B It shows what the countryside looked like as they flew over.

    C It shows how the Montgolfier brothers built their balloon.

    D It shows the size of the balloon and what shape it was.

5. Choose four sentences that should be included in a summary of the passage and number them in the correct order.

—   The first human went up in a balloon on November 21, 1783.

—   The Montgolfiers lived in and performed their experiments in Paris.

—   The first person to fly was French.

—   The Montgolfiers were inspired by a scientific observation.

—   Joseph and Etienne were the Montgolfiers' first names.

—   The first "manned" flight carried a sheep, a rooster, and a duck.

—   The Montgolfiers constructed an envelope to contain hot air.

—   The animals the Montgolfiers sent into the air were not harmed.

6. Choose two inferences you can make about the Montgolfiers and their work based on the information in the passage. Check the box next to each inference you choose.

❏   The Montgolfier brothers were trained as scientists.

❏   Many great inventions started out with an accidental discovery.

❏   People in Paris were interested in the first manned flight.

❏   The smaller the balloon, the harder it is to get it off the ground.

❏   The Montgolfier brothers shared a deep curiosity.

❏   Animals can better withstand air travel than people can.

continued

7. Choose the three most important things the Montgolfiers did in the process of developing lighter-than-air flight and number them in the correct order.

___ Joseph Montgolfier held the neck of a shirt.

___ Two men took the first manned flight in a balloon built by the Montgolfiers.

___ The Montgolfiers figured out that hot air rises.

___ They made the inside of the balloon fireproof.

___ The Montgolfiers launched a "balon" and it flew more than a mile.

___ The Montgolfiers sent up a balloon with three animals as passengers.

8. What evidence does the author use to prove that the Montgolfiers developed lighter-than-air flight? Give at least two details.

_____

_____

_____

_____

_____

9. How did the Montgolfier brothers first "harness hot air's mysterious power"? Use details from the passage to explain how they did it.

_____

_____

_____

_____

_____

continued

10. Describe three historic firsts the Montgolfier brothers achieved and explain what makes these achievements important.

_____

_____

_____

_____

_____

_____

_____

_____

_____

_____

Read the passage. Then answer questions 1–10.

Your Own Coat of Arms

1   You may have seen coats of arms before. These are special pictures or designs that represent a family or group. They may appear on money, on a police badge, or even on the state flag that flies over a school.

2   Coats of arms were first created hundreds of years ago in the Middle Ages. At the time, knights went into battle wearing coats of arms to show what family or castle they fought for. The design from the coat of arms often appeared on the knight's shield too. In a battle, identification on the battlefield was a matter of life or death. The only way to tell armored knights apart was by the emblems on their coats or shields.

3   The art of designing coats of arms is called heraldry. Because of the need for recognition and identification, there are strict rules governing this practice. But anyone can design a coat of arms. For many, the rules make it more fun.

4   If you designed a coat of arms for yourself, what would you put on it? A good coat of arms reveals something special about the wearer. Hobbies, personal history and awards, family legends, and even jokes can all be incorporated into the design. This image is known as the "achievement," and it must fit the rules for designing coats of arms.

I. The Rule of Tincture

5   In heraldry, the most important rule of all is the "rule of tincture." Tinctures are made up of six colors and two metals (silver and gold). Each has its own name from long ago. The rule of tincture is that no color touches a color, and no metal touches a metal. This dramatic contrast makes the image "pop." You can see this rule used in traffic signs, which always have white lettering on a color or black lettering on a metal.

continued

II. Divisions of the Field

6   The design appears on a shield, or field, which may be divided in half lengthwise, horizontally, or diagonally. It may be divided in stripes. The field may be divided in thirds with a triangular wedge at the top or the bottom. The field may also be quartered into four parts. The borders between these divisions do not need to be straight. They may be wavy or jagged, and the background may be checkered or striped.

7   "Ordinaries" offer other possibilities. These are the simplest and oldest designs in heraldry. They include a single stripe, a cross, or a chevron, which is a V-shaped stripe.

8   If your shield is quartered, the tincture rule does not apply. Green, for instance, can be quartered with red. But inside each quarter, the rule does apply. Anything that appears in that quarter must keep the rule of tincture—such as an object, shape, or creature known as the "charge."

Uruguay   Costa Rica   Peru

Honduras   Colombia   Venezuela

III. The Charge

9   Once you've set up your shield, you can place a charge on it. Any object or creature can be the charge. A single, bold charge is best. That makes the achievement clear and clean—the whole point of heraldry.

10   Each charge should mean something. If you create a coat of arms, the charge might be a trophy you won in the third grade, the tree in your front yard, or even the family car. Charges can also stand for ideas. An eagle with its wings spread suggests freedom or bravery. A pen and scroll of paper suggests a writer. Sneakers might suggest a runner.

11   If you do choose an animal, there are different ways to show them. For example, a lion might be shown standing on its back legs and waving its claws, or it might be walking on all fours. On the shield, you could show your cat, your dog, a gecko, or even a pet ferret.

12   Charges may also be geometric shapes or symbols. Circles are common, or you might choose a star, half-moon, or diamond.

IV. The Achievement

13   Remember, the design you create should represent you. Your friends should be able to tell at a glance that the "achievement" stands for you. Then you'll know you have a good coat of arms.

continued

1. In paragraph 5, what does the <u>rule of tincture</u> refer to?

   A ways to fight battles

   B families or special groups

   C colors used in heraldry

   D laws related to knights

2. This question has two parts. Answer Part A first. Then answer Part B.

Part A According to the passage, why were coats of arms invented?

   A to keep knights warm

   B to use for money

   C to help people recognize friends and enemies

   D to decorate castles and homes

Part B Which sentence from the passage supports the answer to Part A?

   A Coats of arms were first created hundreds of years ago in the Middle Ages.

   B The only way to tell armored knights apart was by the emblems on their coats or shields.

   C The art of designing coats of arms is called heraldry.

   D But anyone can design a coat of arms.

3. This question has two parts. Answer Part A first. Then answer Part B.

Part A Which sentence states a main idea of this passage?

   A No color should touch a color, and no metal should touch a metal.

   B The charge on a coat of arms may be an animal, a shape, or a symbol.

   C Coats of arms were first created in the Middle Ages.

   D Using the rules of heraldry, anyone can design a coat of arms.

Part B Which paragraph supports the answer to Part A?

   A paragraph 1

   B paragraph 2

   C paragraph 3

   D paragraph 4

4. According to the passage, where are you likely to see a coat of arms today?

   A on a knight in battle

   B on a state flag

   C on a baseball cap

   D on the side of a truck

continued

5. Based on information in the passage, decide whether each word on the list below is an example of an "ordinary" or a "charge." Write each word in the correct box.

sneakers	chevron	single stripe	diamond
cross	lion	eagle	

Ordinaries	Charges

6. Choose two rules that govern how the field on a coat of arms may be divided, based on the passage. Check the box next to each rule you choose.

☐ No color touches a color.

☐ It may be quartered in four parts.

☐ The animal may be waving its claws or walking on all fours.

☐ The borders between the parts may be straight, wavy, or jagged.

☐ A single, bold charge is best.

☐ It may be a geometric shape or a symbol.

continued

7. What can you tell about coats of arms from the pictures and the passage? Check the box next to each answer you choose.

   ❏   Most of them include something gold.

   ❏   Every coat of arms stands for a family.

   ❏   Shields may be divided in halves, thirds, or quarters.

   ❏   Most coats of arms include geometric symbols.

   ❏   Coats of arms use very bright colors.

   ❏   Most coats of arms include an animal.

8. According to the author, what were "ordinaries," and why were they useful? Give evidence from the passage to support your answer.

_____

_____

_____

_____

_____

9. Explain the importance of the rule of tincture in heraldry. Use at least two details from the passage to support your answer.

_____

_____

_____

_____

_____

continued

10. Describe three rules of heraldry given in the passage, and explain why these rules were most likely created. Use details from the passage in your response.

_____

_____

_____

_____

_____

_____

_____

_____

_____

_____

Short Read 9 • Poetry

Read the passages. Then answer questions 1–10.

from *Rain in Summer*

by Henry Wadsworth Longfellow

How beautiful is the rain!
After the dust and heat,
In the broad and fiery street,
In the narrow lane,
5   How beautiful is the rain!

How it clatters along the roofs,
Like the tramp of hoofs
How it gushes and struggles out
From the throat of the overflowing spout!

10   Across the window-pane
It pours and pours;
And swift and wide,
With a muddy tide,
Like a river down the gutter roars
15   The rain, the welcome rain!

The sick man from his chamber looks
At the twisted brooks;
He can feel the cool
Breath of each little pool;
20   His fevered brain
Grows calm again,
And he breathes a blessing on the rain.

continued

From the neighboring school
Come the boys,
25 With more than their wonted noise
And commotion;
And down the wet streets
Sail their mimic fleets,
Till the treacherous pool
30 Ingulfs them in its whirling
And turbulent ocean.

In the country, on every side,
Where far and wide,
Like a leopard's tawny and spotted hide,
35 Stretches the plain,
To the dry grass and the drier grain
How welcome is the rain! . . .

The Rainy Morning

by James Whitcomb Riley

The dawn of the day was dreary,
And the lowering clouds o'erhead
Wept in a silent sorrow
Where the sweet sunshine lay dead;
5 And a wind came out of the eastward
Like an endless sigh of pain,
And the leaves fell down in the pathway
And writhed in the falling rain.

I had tried in a brave endeavor
10 To chord my harp with the sun,
But the strings would slacken ever,
And the task was a weary one:
And so, like a child impatient
And sick of a discontent,
15 I bowed in a shower of teardrops
And mourned with the instrument.

And lo! as I bowed, the splendor
Of the sun bent over me,
With a touch as warm and tender
20 As a father's hand might be:
And even as I felt its presence,
My clouded soul grew bright,
And the tears, like the rain of morning,
Melted in mists of light.

continued ➔

1. Read these lines from "Rain in Summer."

> How beautiful is the rain!
>
> How it clatters along the roofs,
>
> Like the tramp of hoofs

What do these lines mean?

- **A** The rain sounds like horses' hooves.
- **B** The rain is so loud that it wakes the poet.
- **C** There are animals on the roof.
- **D** Horses are riding by in the rain.

2. This question has two parts. Answer Part A first. Then answer Part B.

Part A What is a central idea in "Rain in Summer"?

    A The world would be better off without rain.

    B Rain makes people feel better.

    C People should go outside and enjoy the rain.

    D Rain acts like a group of boys.

Part B Which lines from the poem support the answer to Part A?

    A After the dust and heat
        In the broad and fiery street,

    B How it gushes and struggles out
        From the throat of the overflowing spout!

    C His fevered brain
        Grows calm again,

    D From the neighboring school
        Come the boys,

continued

3. This question has two parts. Answer Part A first. Then answer Part B.

Part A In "The Rainy Morning," what does the word <u>dreary</u> mean in line 1?

  A cheerful

  B slow

  C gloomy

  D quiet

Part B Choose two phrases from the poem that help you understand the meaning of the word <u>dreary</u>. Check the box next to each phrase you choose.

  ❑ The dawn of the day

  ❑ the lowering clouds

  ❑ Wept in a silent sorrow

  ❑ sweet sunshine

  ❑ And a wind

  ❑ out of the eastward

4. What is the general theme and mood in the first two stanzas of "The Rainy Morning"?

  A The cheerful sun is the father of rain.

  B A rainy day can make you feel sad.

  C When you're unhappy, it always seems to be raining.

  D Rain is better than sunshine.

5. Which elements can be found in "Rain in Summer," in "The Rainy Morning," or in both? In the box next to each sentence, write either 1 for "Rain in Summer," 2 for "The Rainy Morning," or 3 for both.

The poem contains figures of speech that compare different things.	
All of the stanzas are the same length.	
All of the lines have a similar rhythm.	
Some lines are repeated.	
Many lines rhyme.	
All of the lines have the same meter, or pattern of stressed syllables.	

continued

6. What can you infer about the speaker in "The Rainy Morning"?
   Check the box next to each inference you choose.

   ☐   Clouds make the speaker dream of faraway places.

   ☐   Music usually cheers up the speaker.

   ☐   The speaker does not know how to play the harp.

   ☐   To the speaker, the clouds seem to be crying.

   ☐   Playing the harp always makes the speaker cry.

   ☐   The east wind makes the speaker feel better.

7. In which lines from "Rain in Summer" does the poet compare
   something to an animal? Check the box next to each example
   you choose.

   ☐   How it clatters along the roofs,
        Like the tramp of hoofs

   ☐   How it gushes and struggles out
        From the throat of the overflowing spout!

   ☐   Like a river down the gutter roars
        The rain, the welcome rain!

   ☐   And down the wet streets
        Sail their mimic fleets,

   ☐   Like a leopard's tawny and spotted hide,
        Stretches the plain,

   ☐   To the dry grass and the drier grain
        How welcome is the rain!

8. Compare and contrast how the two poems present rain. Use details from each poem in your answer.

_____

_____

_____

_____

_____

_____

9. Compare and contrast the speakers' points of view in "Rain in Summer" and "The Rainy Morning." Include details from the poems in your answer.

_____

_____

_____

_____

_____

continued

10. What change does the speaker experience in "The Rainy Morning"?
Use at least three details from the poem in your answer.

_____

_____

_____

_____

_____

_____

_____

_____

_____

_____

Read the passages. Then answer questions 1–10.

The Chariot Driver of Qi

1   Once there lived in the province of Qi, in China, a very proud chariot driver. His job was to take the prime minister from place to place on business. Whenever the driver got up behind his horses, the majesty of his wonderful job transformed him. His smile beamed like a thousand suns. But he could glower, too, if anyone crossed his path while he was on duty. Most of all, the driver liked to hold his head up high with an arrogant sneer. The look seemed to show disdain for everyone alive.

2   Of course, when he went home each night to his wife, he was as humble as anyone else. If anything, he was humbler. He never said a word about his job or how he felt about it.

3   The driver's downfall came when, one day, the prime minister had important business that took him through the driver's own village. The driver sped through the streets, cracking his whip. He looked prouder than ever as he showed off to his neighbors. One of the neighbors ran excitedly to the home of the driver's wife, shouting, "Come see! Come see! Your husband is driving the prime minister!"

continued ➡

4   As the chariot rumbled past, the driver straightened up and shot his nose into the air with the snobbiest look he had ever managed.

5   That night, his wife didn't say a word to him.

6   Nothing at all.

7   "What have I done?" he asked, to end her silence. "Why are you not happy?"

8   She simply told him she was going home to live with her mother. When he pressed her for a reason, she finally explained.

9   "When I saw you next to the prime minister, he was the model of modesty and dignity. Next to him, your airs and pretentiousness looked ridiculous. You, a mere driver, were acting haughtier than the highest official in the land. This is why I must leave—I don't want to have a ridiculous husband."

10   The driver returned to his job more than a little humbled. Crisscrossing Qi on country roads and lonely highways gave him plenty of time to think. As he did so, his face got longer and more serious, but also less arrogant. He missed his wife!

11   One day the minister asked him about his new attitude.

12   "You have clearly changed your behavior, my man. May I ask why?"

13   "My wife left me because of my arrogance," the man said honestly. "And now that I've had time to think about it, I know she was right."

14   The minister was very impressed. Such a change, he knew, was hardly easy to accomplish. He took the driver to the king and explained all that had happened.

15   "My driver is a man of virtue," he said. "He has the courage to correct his mistakes."

16   The king instantly saw that the driver was indeed a man of character.

17   "I shall raise you to the rank of officer at my court," the king proclaimed.

18   The man went back to his wife, who received him with great joy, saying, "The fine, modest man I married has returned!"

19   From that point on, the man who had once driven the prime minister's chariot fulfilled his duties with humility. Both he and his wife lived happily ever after.

continued

The Girl Who Saved the Village

1   Long, long ago, there stood a small and humble village in the valley of a great mountain. The people of the village had no riches, but they had golden fields of wheat and emerald hills of grass for their sheep, so they were happy.

2   But one day, when the sun goddess Sola chose the top of their mountain as her new home, the rain stopped falling. A drought descended upon the village like a nightmare from which no one could awaken. Without wheat to bake bread, the villagers became weak. Without lush grass to eat, the sheep became sickly. The people were becoming desperate. But just as it is sometimes darkest before the dawn, a baby girl named Sage was born.

3   From the moment of her birth, it was clear that Sage was unique. "She seems to radiate with pure delight, just like the sun!" her father would brag, and it was true. As she grew up, villagers would go out of their way just to stand near Sage. They loved to feel her powerful joy warm their heart like the rays of the sun.

4   Sadly, Sage's parents' love for their daughter turned into a poisonous pride. As she grew older, they began to believe that their daughter was superior. "She will achieve what no one else can, you'll see," her father boasted. He became obsessed with the glory Sage would surely bring. No one was surprised when he declared that Sage was going up the mountain to confront Sola.

5   "Order Sola to leave, Sage," her mother said, "and we will be royalty in this dusty little village!"

6   With a heavy heart, Sage set out for the mountain. She climbed until she came to a garden filled with strange flowers that seemed to flicker like flames. A tiny woman sat at the edge of a small pond. She was watching tiny, ruby-red fish swim in circles. "Hello, traveler," said the woman. "What brings you to this place above the clouds?"

7   Sage sighed. "I have come to ask the sun goddess to leave. My village has been suffering from a drought for a long time, and if she does not move from this mountain, everything and everyone will die."

8   "Oh, I'm sure Sola was not aware of your suffering!" said the woman. "You've asked so politely that Sola surely will agree to visit the other mountains of the world. But why are you still troubled?"

9   "I'm glad the drought will end, but my success brings another kind of trouble. My parents will expect to live as royalty now. Their pride has made them forget who they are."

10   The tiny woman then stood. It was Sola herself! A blazing white light surrounded her. The garden air seemed to shimmer. With a kind but sad voice she spoke. "Sage, I will leave this mountain and the rains will fall. But a new drought will begin—a drought of the heart. Your parents will gain glory, but they will lose what is truly important—humility, love, and you. You will be like a stranger to them. Only when they become aware of their folly and change their foolish ways will they recognize you as their beloved daughter once again. May it not take them long."

11   With those words, Sola rose and streaked across the sky like a kite of blinding white fire. Almost immediately, the rain began to fall, and Sage started trudging toward home. The valley would soon turn green and there would be plenty of food for all. But for the first time in her life, Sage could not smile.

continued

1. Which sentence expresses the theme of "The Chariot Driver of Qi"?

    A Some people are born to rule.

    B Your real character comes out when you think no one is watching.

    C A little caution goes a long way.

    D Be true to who you are.

2. This question has two parts. Answer Part A first. Then answer Part B.

Part A In "The Chariot Driver of Qi," what is the meaning of the word <u>disdain</u> as it is used in paragraph 1?

    A deep pride in one's achievements

    B a feeling of scorn toward those who are unworthy

    C warm friendship and affection for others

    D a lack of respect for those who are superior

Part B Which phrase from paragraph 1 helps you understand the meaning of <u>disdain</u>?

    A Most of all, the driver

    B with an arrogant sneer

    C seemed to show

    D for everyone alive

3. This question has two parts. Answer Part A first. Then answer Part B.

Part A In "The Chariot Driver of Qi," how does the driver's attitude change from the beginning to the end of the passage?

  A At first he loves his wife, but later he loses patience with her.

  B At first he acts arrogant when he drives, but later he is more humble.

  C At first he is unskilled as a driver, but later he drives like an experienced professional.

  D At first he is proud to drive the prime minister, but later he wants a better job.

Part B Which sentence from the passage signals the change indicated in the answer to Part A?

  A As he did so, his face got longer and more serious, but also less arrogant.

  B Of course, when he went home each night to his wife, he was as humble as anyone else.

  C As the chariot rumbled past, the driver straightened up and shot his nose into the air with the snobbiest look he had ever managed.

  D "You, a mere driver, were acting haughtier than the highest official in the land."

continued

4. Read the sentence from "The Girl Who Saved the Village."

> But just as it is sometimes darkest before the dawn, a baby girl named Sage was born.

What does the phrase "darkest before the dawn" suggest about this moment for the villagers?

A Life is the most difficult just before it gets better.

B The moon and stars become invisible just before the sun rises.

C The villagers need lanterns when walking just before dawn.

D Just when life gets better, it becomes more difficult again.

5. Choose two inferences you can make about Sage in "The Girl Who Saved the Village." Check the box next to each inference you choose.

☐ She was proud of her beauty and her parents.

☐ She did not want to confront the sun goddess.

☐ She wanted to be treated as a queen for saving the village.

☐ She did not think her parents really deserved to live like royalty.

☐ She had always secretly wanted to be a goddess.

☐ She only felt good when she was close to important people.

6. If "The Girl Who Saved the Village" were written as a play, which three elements would be added? Check the box next to each of the elements you choose.

- ❏ cast of characters

- ❏ dialogue

- ❏ stanzas

- ❏ plot

- ❏ stage directions

- ❏ verse

- ❏ scenes or acts

continued ➡

7. Choose four sentences that should be included in a summary of "The Chariot Driver of Qi" and number them in the correct order.

— The chariot driver crisscrosses Qi on lonely roads.

— The king gives the chariot driver a position at court.

— The chariot driver's wife leaves him for being arrogant.

— The chariot driver speeds through the streets.

— The prime minister sees that the chariot driver's attitude has changed.

— A neighbor of the chariot driver runs yelling through the streets.

— The prime minister's chariot driver is proud of his job and looks down on others.

— When the chariot driver gets home, his wife says nothing to him.

8. In "The Girl Who Saved the Village," why did Sage go to the top of the mountain? Use two or more details from the passage to support your answer.

_____

_____

_____

_____

_____

9. How does the illustration in "The Chariot Driver of Qi" add to the reader's enjoyment and understanding of the story? Give two examples.

_____

_____

_____

_____

_____

continued ▶

10. How are these two stories similar in theme and plot, and how are they different? Give at least two similarities and two differences in your response.

_____

_____

_____

_____

_____

_____

_____

_____

_____

_____

_____

Read the passages. Then answer questions 1–10.

How to Build a Japanese Fighter Kite

1   The people of Japan have been building fighter kites for hundreds of years. Now you, too, can build a Japanese kite.

2   Fighter kites are maneuverable, single-line kites, very much like the kind you may have flown yourself. Most kites use a long tail to keep stable. Fighting kites, on the other hand, are all about movement and maneuverability. They are designed to respond sharply to each tug on the line.

3   As you practice controlling a fighter kite, you'll discover how the kite becomes a living thing. The more practice you get, the clearer it will be that tugs on the line are a language all their own. Mastering a fighter kite takes constant focus and deft fingers. After much practice, you may discover skills you never knew you had. Some people find kite-flying very restful, too, because focusing on the kite helps clear your mind of other thoughts or worries.

Kite Components

4   Today most fighting kites are basically square or diamond-shaped. Historically, though, they came in every shape and size. No matter what the shape, the basic scientific principles of flight influence the design.

5   What are the key features of a fighter kite? The kite's basic fabric is called the sail. The sail can be made of anything from newspaper to nylon to high-tech plastic. The material simply needs to be light and strong with a smooth surface.

6   You need a frame to stretch the sail. The backbone of this frame is a rigid stick called the spine. The spine stiffens the kite from top to bottom.

continued

7   The next part of the fighter's frame is a horizontal stick called the cross spar. The spar spreads the sail from side to side. Spars can be made of wood, bamboo, fiberglass, or even carbon fiber. The ends of the spar fit into fabric pockets to attach to the sail. These pockets help bend the spar, giving it a bow-like shape that keeps the sail stiff and flat. The bend improves stability.

8   The lines that attach to the kite are called bridle lines. There might be two or three of these. They attach to the single flying line at what is called the tow-point. The placement of the bridle points, or connections, creates the angle at which the kite faces the wind. The bridle lines also spread the wind's force across the kite's frame, giving it more stability.

9   Fighters can have other features, such as holes in the sail, tails, or stiffening sticks called battens. Kites may be decorated with bright colors or symbols, too, or they may be plain. But the model described here has all the basic features you'll need in your first fighter kite.

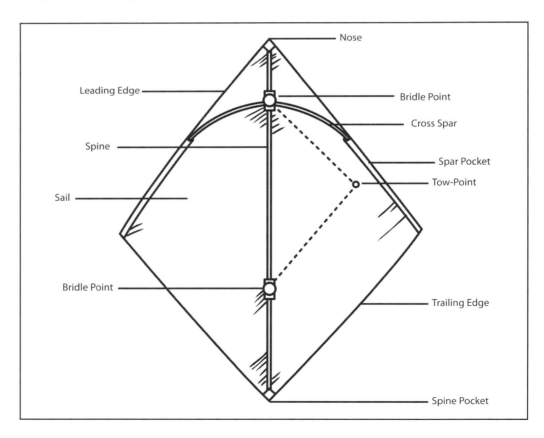

A History of Japanese Kites

10 Over the past two thousand years, kite-flying traditions have popped up in every corner of the globe. Kites are flown in China, Thailand, Korea, India, Malaysia, and even, most recently, Brazil. But for elegant lines, beautiful decorations, and even sheer size, no kites match the fighter kites of Japan. Each kite is a work of art, built by a master craftsman. The kites are part of a history that reaches back to the country's earliest days.

11 In China, the kite had a number of practical uses, such as sending signals to other towns or communicating with neighbors. As other cultures adopted kites, the practice of kite-fighting arose. Many believe that kite fighting happened first in India. Then early Dutch traders who saw the kites in India took the practice to Nagasaki, Japan.

12 Today people remember Japan's kite history largely through kite-fighting festivals. These are held throughout the nation at different times of year. Like the kites themselves, the festivals come in all sizes and shapes. For example, the city of Nagasaki has a month-long kite festival every March.

13 One of the most famous festivals takes place in the first week of May in Hamamatsu. In a tradition that goes back to the 1500s, each of the town's 164 blocks is represented by a single kite. This kite carries the mark for that particular block. Some of these kites are enormous. They can measure as much as twelve feet on a side. To keep stable, these kites need tails as long as fifteen or twenty times the size of the kite itself.

14 Each fighting kite is flown by a team of men. The goal of the kite fighter is to cut the strings of the other kites. To do this, each kite's line is covered with a mix of glue and ground glass. When a kite's line is cut, the fun begins. Team members and onlookers chase the free-floating kite to wherever it lands. Whoever gets to it first may claim the kite.

15 As many as two million people a year visit the Hamamatsu festival. Other kite-fighting festivals across Japan draw smaller crowds. And just as the Hamamatsu festival gave rise to its own style of kite, so do the other festivals. There are dozens of shapes, sizes, and designs.

continued

1. This question has two parts. Answer Part A first. Then answer Part B.

Part A In "How to Build a Japanese Fighter Kite," what is the meaning of the word <u>deft</u> in paragraph 3?

    A relaxed and comfortable

    B sore; painful

    C light and quick in movement

    D strong; muscular

Part B Which phrase from paragraph 3 helps you understand the meaning of <u>deft</u>?

    A controlling a fighter kite

    B a living thing

    C a language all their own

    D skills you never knew you had

2. According to "How to Build a Japanese Fighter Kite," which of these features would make a fighter kite more stable?

    A longer tail

    B flatter cross spar

    C fewer bridle points

    D lighter sail material

3. This question has two parts. Answer Part A first. Then answer Part B.

Part A Which sentence states the main idea of fighter kite design, according to "How to Build a Japanese Fighter Kite"?

   A   Most kites use a long tail to keep stable.

   B   Fighting kites, on the other hand, are all about movement and maneuverability.

   C   As you practice controlling a fighter kite, you'll discover how the kite becomes a living thing.

   D   Over the past two thousand years, kite-flying traditions have popped up in every corner of the globe.

Part B Which sentence from the passage best supports the answer to Part A?

   A   The people of Japan have been building fighter kites for hundreds of years.

   B   They are designed to respond sharply to each tug on the line.

   C   After much practice, you may discover skills you never knew you had.

   D   Today most fighting kites are basically square or diamond-shaped.

continued

4. According to the illustration, what holds the sail to the spine and the cross spar?

    A the guiding line

    B pockets

    C bridle points

    D the frame

5. Choose three features shown in the diagram that add to a fighter kite's stability. Check the box next to each feature you choose.

    ❑ the curve of the cross spar

    ❑ the material in the spine

    ❑ the absence of a tail

    ❑ the placement of the bridle points

    ❑ the cross spar-and-spine frame

    ❑ the dimensions of the sail

6. Choose three details from "A History of Japanese Kites" supporting the idea that kites are an important part of Japanese culture. Check the box next to each detail you choose.

❏   Over the past two thousand years, kite-flying traditions have popped up in every corner of the globe.

❏   But for elegant lines, beautiful decorations, and even sheer size, no kites match the fighter kites of Japan.

❏   In a tradition that goes back to the 1500s, each of the town's 164 blocks is represented by a single kite.

❏   There are dozens of shapes, sizes, and designs.

❏   Team members and onlookers chase the free-floating kite to wherever it lands.

❏   As many as two million people a year visit the Hamamatsu festival.

❏   Then early Dutch traders who saw the kites in India took the practice to Nagasaki, Japan.

continued

7. Choose four sentences to summarize the history of Japanese kites and number them in the correct order.

—— India began a fighting kite tradition.

—— China started flying kites with practical uses.

—— Japan's Hamamatsu festival began.

—— Today Japan has kite-flying festivals all over the country.

—— Brazil began kite fighting.

—— Dutch traders brought kite fighting to Japan.

—— A month-long kite festival was held in Nagasaki, Japan.

8. According to "A History of Japanese Kites," if you were watching two men fighting with kites, what would you see them do? Use details from the passage to support your answer.

_____

_____

_____

_____

_____

_____

9. Describe the basic shape, appearance, and parts of a fighter kite. Use details from "How to Build a Japanese Fighter Kite" and the diagram to support your answer.

_____

_____

_____

_____

_____

_____

continued

10. Explain how the author shows that kite fighting is an old and strong tradition in Japan. Use at least three examples or details from the passages in your response.

_____

_____

_____

_____

_____

_____

_____

_____

_____

_____

Read the passage. Then answer questions 1–10.

The Silk Road

1   The world's first great trade route was the Silk Road. It was a network of roads and trails stretching thousands of miles across Asia. Branches of the Silk Road passed through mountain ranges, deserts, and broad grasslands. Over time, these paths linked the great cities of the Middle East to faraway China.

2   The Silk Road didn't spring up overnight. It developed over hundreds and hundreds of years. Small trails connected, producing longer trails. Traders journeyed along these varied paths to buy and sell their goods. As trade grew, new trails and new roads became connected to the Silk Road, and the trade route expanded.

Tough Travel

3   A journey on the Silk Road could be difficult, dangerous, and slow. Trails passed through sandy deserts and harsh mountain passes. Many traders traveled in caravans for safety. Merchants and guards, missionaries and pilgrims trekked together on the road. Going with a group gave some protection from bandits and soldiers.

4   The main pack animals were camels. They could go long distances without water and live on shrubs and thorny bushes. They could also carry huge loads, up to 500 pounds. But these sturdy animals covered only about thirty miles per day.

continued ▶

Varied Goods

5   The name of the Silk Road highlights the most important good sold along the route: Chinese silk. Demand for this commodity made silk very valuable, and people traveled thousands of miles to get it. Outside of China, nobody knew how to produce silk. Chinese officials tried to keep silk production a secret. Eventually, spies discovered that silk comes from silkworms, which eat the leaves of mulberry trees. The silkworms spin cocoons that can be made into silk products. In time, people began to make silk in other lands.

6   Many other goods moved along the Silk Road from many different places. Caravans and camels transported spices, nuts, dates, tea, and other food products. Their loads also contained gold, precious stones, porcelain, and glassware. Merchants traded horses and cattle, as well.

Other Exchanges

7   Goods were not the only important exchanges that took place because of the Silk Road. Travelers entertained each other, traded ideas, and swapped information along the road. They shared stories, music, art, and dance. These art forms, like trade goods, passed from place to place. Sometimes tales, music, and art changed in new settings or mingled with local arts.

8   Similarly, travelers traded new skills, tools, and inventions. They shared new methods for farming and fighting. Paper money, compasses, and gunpowder, for example, were all Chinese inventions. People who traveled to China surely brought some of these ideas and products back with them.

9   Religion was also transmitted from traveler to traveler along the Silk Road. Buddhism started in India and spread across China and into central Asia. Later, Islam extended from northern Africa into central Asia by way of the trade routes.

Endings and Beginnings

10 By the late 1400s, trade was declining on the Silk Road.
    Explorers from Europe, such as Christopher Columbus, began
    to search for better and faster sea routes to Asia. Eventually,
    new maritime routes replaced the great land route, and the Silk
    Road faded away.

The Silk Road

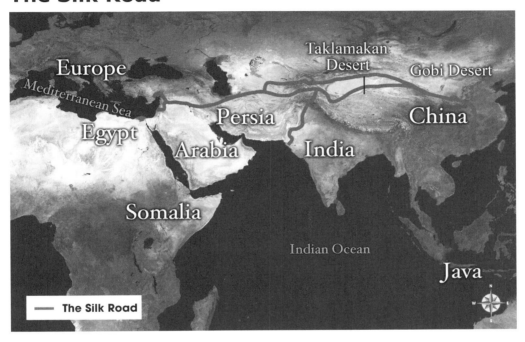

continued ➤

Sailing to Asia

1   Does the name Marco Polo sound familiar? He is one of the most famous explorers in history. In the early 1300s, he became one of the first Europeans to travel across the lands stretching from Italy to China. He played an important role in the establishment of the Silk Road. But there is another important European explorer you may not know about: Vasco da Gama. What Marco Polo accomplished on foot, da Gama accomplished on water. Vasco da Gama was the first explorer to sail from Europe to India.

2   The Silk Road helped merchants trade goods between European, Middle Eastern, and Asian nations. But the Silk Road was a long and dangerous route. There were mountains to climb, deserts to cross, and bandits to avoid. Camels were used to carry goods, and this limited the amount a merchant could trade. Leaders in many nations longed for an ocean route that would make trading easier.

3   On July 8, 1497, Vasco da Gama and his crew left Lisbon, Portugal, with four ships. They sailed southward around Africa's Cape of Good Hope and then northward toward India. On May 20, 1498, da Gama arrived in Calicut, India. He and his crew were the first Europeans to sail all the way to Asia! By doing so, da Gama proved that Europeans could reach Asia by sailing around Africa. His next goal was to build a trade station for Portugal in India.

4   At first, the people of India welcomed da Gama and his men with celebrations and feasts. But this friendliness did not last long. The Hindu king feared that if he allowed Portugal to build a trade station, he would anger merchants from other countries. So he refused. Da Gama was disappointed, but what could he do? He decided to lead his men back home.

5   When da Gama arrived back in Portugal, he received a hero's welcome. The king rewarded him with money and made him an admiral. Da Gama had learned a lot during the trip and wanted to try again. In February of 1502, da Gama set sail for India as a viceroy for the king of Portugal. As an official representative of the king, he was finally allowed to build a trade center. An ocean trade route between Europe and Asia was established.

6   After da Gama's successful voyages, many other countries followed suit. People throughout Europe, Africa, and Asia benefited greatly from this trade and exploration. Goods, technologies, and ideas spread to more areas and at a faster rate than along the Silk Road. The world was changed forever. Da Gama and Marco Polo may have taken different paths, but both changed the world in astounding ways.

continued

1. This question has two parts. Answer Part A first. Then answer Part B.

Part A Which sentence states a main idea of "The Silk Road"?

A The main pack animals were camels.

B The name of the Silk Road highlights the most important good sold along the route: Chinese silk.

C Paper money, compasses, and gunpowder, for example, were all Chinese inventions.

D Explorers from Europe, such as Christopher Columbus, began to search for better and faster sea routes to Asia.

Part B Which sentence from the passage supports the answer to Part A?

A But these sturdy animals covered only about thirty miles per day.

B Buddhism started in India and spread across China and into central Asia.

C Demand for this commodity made silk very valuable, and people traveled thousands of miles to get it.

D Caravans and camels transported spices, nuts, dates, tea, and other food products.

2. What text structure does the author use to organize most of the information in "Sailing to Asia"?

  A cause and effect

  B order of importance

  C problem and solution

  D chronological order

3. This question has two parts. Answer Part A first. Then answer Part B.

Part A In "The Silk Road," what does the word <u>commodity</u> mean in paragraph 5?

  A a product to be traded

  B a form of transportation

  C an unusual creature

  D a foreign country

Part B Which phrase from paragraph 5 helps you understand the meaning of <u>commodity</u>?

  A The name of the Silk Road

  B highlights the most important

  C good sold along the route

  D traveled thousands of miles

continued

4. What inference about Vasco da Gama can be drawn from the information in "Sailing to Asia"?

   A He wanted to live in India.

   B He did not give up easily.

   C He spoke a number of languages.

   D His dream was to become an admiral.

5. In "The Silk Road," what reasons does the author give to support the idea that silk was the main reason for the Silk Road? Check the box next to each reason you choose.

   ❏ The world's first great trade route was the Silk Road.

   ❏ Silk was the most important good sold along the route.

   ❏ Spies found out that silk came from silkworms.

   ❏ Many other goods moved along the Silk Road.

   ❏ The Chinese did not want anyone to know how silk was made.

   ❏ European explorers searched for better routes to Asia.

6. Based on "Sailing to Asia," why were Vasco da Gama's voyages so important? Choose three reasons. Check the box next to the reasons you choose.

- ☐   Da Gama opened a trade route between Italy and China.

- ☐   He brought new inventions from China, such as gunpowder and paper money.

- ☐   He proved that Europeans could sail to Asia by going around Africa.

- ☐   Da Gama's voyages helped spread ideas and technologies around the world.

- ☐   He introduced the Hindu religion from India to people in Europe.

- ☐   He helped India become a world power as an ally to Portugal.

- ☐   He established a European trade center in India.

continued ➤

7. Choose three things you can learn from the map of the Silk Road. Check the box next to each answer you choose.

❏   The Silk Road extended the length of Africa.

❏   From the Silk Road, explorers sailed to ports in Asia.

❏   The Silk Road connected Europe and Asia.

❏   The Silk Road ended in Tehran.

❏   The Silk Road crossed two major deserts.

❏   From the Silk Road, travelers could go to India.

❏   The Silk Road crossed two oceans.

8. According to "The Silk Road," why did merchants travel in caravans on the Silk Road? Give two reasons.

_____

_____

_____

_____

_____

9. According to the author of "Sailing to Asia," why was an ocean trade route between Europe and Asia better than a land trade route? Give two reasons.

_____

_____

_____

_____

_____

continued

10. Why was the Silk Road so important, and how was it replaced? Use at least two details from each passage to support your answer.

_____

_____

_____

_____

_____

_____

_____

_____

_____

_____

Notes

Notes

Notes

Notes

Notes

_____

_____

_____

_____

_____

_____

_____

_____

_____

_____

_____

_____

_____

Notes